# God is Love

**DR KRISHNA SAKSENA**

*Published by*
**PRABHAT PRAKASHAN PVT. LTD.**
4/19 Asaf Ali Road,
New Delhi-110002 (INDIA)
e-mail: prabhatbooks@gmail.com

ISBN 978-93-5521-796-7

**GOD IS LOVE**
*by* Dr Krishna Saksena



*Edition*
First, 2023

*Price*
₹ 250 (Rupees Two Hundred Only)

*Printed at*
Japan Art, Delhi

# Preface

Exploring the Divine Essence.

Welcome to a journey of faith, where the author delves into the profound concept that has echoed through the ages: "God is Love." In this exploration, she embarks on a quest to understand the essence of the Divine, a force that has captivated the hearts and minds of humanity for millennia.

Throughout history, countless individuals have sought to comprehend the nature of God and the meaning of love. From ancient scriptures to modern reflections, from theological treatises to personal testimonies, the concept of God's love has been interpreted, contemplated, and celebrated in diverse ways.

In this book, the author approaches the topic with reverence, curiosity, and an open heart. She reflects on the idea that love is not merely an attribute of God, but the very essence of God's being. She considers how this understanding shapes our perspectives on faith, spirituality, and the human experience.

Through these pages, we will explore the many facets of God's love. We reflect on the unconditional love that embraces all beings, the redemptive love that offers forgiveness and grace, the compassionate love that heals and comforts, and the transformative love that inspires us to be our best selves. We ponder the challenges and complexities of understanding and experiencing God's love in a world filled with suffering, doubt, and questions.

As we journey through these contemplations, we do so with humility, recognising that our understanding of God's love is shaped by our personal beliefs, experiences, and perspectives. We honour the diversity of beliefs and interpretations that exist within different faith traditions and seek to engage in a respectful and open-minded exploration.

It is my hope that this book will serve as a source of inspiration, encouragement, and reflection for all who read it. May it ignite our soul with the awareness of God's ever-present love, and may it deepen our understanding of the Divine essence that permeates all of creation.

In closing, I express my gratitude for the author to share her exploration with us, dear readers. May our shared journey through the pages of this book be a catalyst for deeper insights, meaningful conversations, and a profound connection with the boundless love that emanates from the Divine. May it inspire you as it has inspired me.

–**Dr. Ajay Gupta**

*An eminent academician*
*and a renowned*
*Orthopedic Surgeon*

## God is love

It is the right man that can save the world. Which is standing on the verge of disaster. Are you the right man? A basic question that needs to be addressed by every individual. Sooner than later this question will confront you. What is your answer?

Let me start with an interesting story. A father gave a map of the world torn into pieces spread on a plate and asked his son to put it right. The son took the torn pieces and within a period of four minutes, he brought the plate with each piece at its right place. The father was taken aback for he himself could not have done so fast and so accurately and within such a short time. He was hesitant in asking the son but he could not stop himself. He asked his son, "How could you do it so fast?" The child replied, "At the back of the pieces of paper is the figure of a man. I put the man right and thus the world was right."

I wonder what kind of love is that to another yet to another it can shift. We are always running most of the time in our lives facing disappointments. What we need to do is to take a breath, stop and think and then resume our run without focusing on discussions. What we must do is to take a practical approach to our problems. I have lived a long life of 92 years so I can share and talk about yours and my problems. Our entire life is a continuous process of learning. Any process of enquiry should be concerned with finding out what is transient and what is permanent. This is true knowledge. Goodness is achieved not in a vacuum but in the company of other men attended by love.

See the lovely lotus as it blooms and spreads its scent all round and touches every heart, resounds gracefully with the rhythm that God is love, love is God.

Does your inner voice talk to you? Call it Divine mind or intuition that never leads you astray. What is more, you can actually develop intuitive powers. Some would call the source God, some the Supreme light. While, some would call it the accumulated wisdom of our many births. We are always on the run, even from ourselves. In the race, there is nothing but only great ambitions followed by disappointments and frustration. We live a life of discontent, devoid of happiness. Here in is a clarion call for all those who wish to take a breath, stop, think and then perhaps resume their run.

The greatest hindrance on the path of love is your own ego. It is difficult to kill it. We have only the right to work. It is the ego in us that yearns for returns. I have done so much for this fellow and he has never thought of doing anything for me. It is "me" and "I"that is hurt. A proper war has to be raged against ego, the one great hindrance on the path of love. But let your ego answer that you are the servant of the Divine power and you are here to serve others and serve the Lord. Such ego will spread love all round.

A beautiful building is built on strong stones that have ego and pride on themselves that the building stands on them and even if one brick thinks of moving out, the building will tumble down. A crow sitting next to it looks at the building that is up high and feels happy that one day he will sit high when the building is completed and so humbly, he gives his contribution by bringing some little material in his peak. He will, when the building is complete happily sing in the praises of the Lord. The crow has no ego and so he is happy. Watch a small child smiling and you are enchanted. Be a child before you realise this. You may have immense wealth but you may be running away from happiness.

A proper war has to be waged against egoism, the greatest hindrance to love. Happiness should not elate and sorrows should not depress you. God is love and love is God. Love is great. It is God-like. Meditation, God, and love does not require any specific age or time. "It is God like for being loved by someone. It gives you strength, loving someone deeply gives you courage."

I am a devotee of Divine Mother. So, I went on a visit to all the different shrines of Ma and was very happy on return. I felt I had made a great achievement. Immense happiness was in my heart. Next day, I took my bath and came into my Puja room and put my head on Her feet and thanked Her for all that She had shown and taught me when I felt a heavy pat on my back. No one was in the house. I thought some mud had fallen from the roof. My reaction was that I got up to see as to what could be there but everything was just intact. I sat down again with folded hands when a dupatta touching my cheeks passed over my head. I was sure that it was my Divine Mother running out. I smiled and thanked Her. In troubles or in doubts, it is to you MA that I always look to. Whenever I am ill, the whispering sound of the wind going over the flowers make me regain my health. Laughing or crying you are always there. I am your child. In laughter or in my cries, I see you and only you.

On the death of my husband, I went mad and the one whom I loved so much, I threw Her out not only from my heart but also out of my house and as I was shifting to another accommodation, I told the labourers shifting my luggage not to carry my Divine Mother and all Her photographs and idols. I got highly disturbed. I went to the college but could not do justice to the students. At night, I lay in my bed with eyes wide open. Disturbed and confused, I looked so silly when I looked at my face in the mirror. My son was very anxious about me and took me to a number of psychiatrists but nothing seemed to work.

One day vacantly sitting, I noticed lot of mud under the bed of Shiv, my youngest son. It came to my mind to take it out so the servant would pick up and throw it out. With this intention in mind, I went to get a broom. Quite a number of brooms were packed up on a shelf. I started searching. Some red colour was shining from below. Hurriedly, I threw the brooms covering it and to my surprise it was none but my

Mother Divine. She said, "I could not leave you." I cleaned Her and put Her on a shelf on which I spread a satin cloth. Tears came in my eyes and I told the Mother, "I am sorry. Ma always forgives. I thank you Ma for being so loving and so kind."

Love never knows what it gains. It sacrifices life at its altar. It rises much above sex. Sex may be the outcome of love but never the cause of it. This is Indian culture.

In many ways, our arranged marriage is much better than what the West has.

A man asked the sage:

*"Should I give up every thing like you to live a life of honesty and truthfulness."*

The sage replied:

*"Not at all. What you need to understand is that you can find and follow the path of unselfishness, you will find happiness and peace.*

*If you are going to keep your wealth, it is better to throw it away than let it poison your heart. But if you do not cling to it and use it wisely then you will be a blessing to the people.*

Love gave us such high figures like Savarkar who for the love of his country begged for his death than Black Water punishment. His happiness was in death as this penalty would give him life to work and serve his country.

Such great men have been here in India. What you have to understand is that your actions are the ones that determine your life. How you act will decide what type of a person you are.

Near the river is a vast ground where religious discourses, discussions, lectures, etc. were held and sadhus, great religious figures, come of and on to teach that "whatever you do, do it in the spirit that it is a prayer to the Lord." Men hear all this and feel they are highly religious. But coming out of the gate of the ground, they see a man lying down on the ground profusely bleeding at being hit by a scooter rickshaw, they turn their face the other way and go off. It was an old illiterate lady walking on the other side who saw him from a distance and who came over to him, got hold of his begging hand and slowly took him to his place.

"Who is working as a devotee to the Lord?" The answer is clear!

Ramesh and Suresh were friends. So were their sons Shyam and Ram. Once, it so happened that Ram's mother fell seriously ill so Ramesh requested his friend to keep his son for a week so that he could go to see her. The friend readily agreed. He was very poor but the share of milk of his child he gave it to the child of his friend. This is how true friends feel for each other despite their disparity.

We have been sent here not to renounce but to rejoice. Actions are most important. God has sent us so that we may act with love. How can you think of leaving this world and sitting in a jungle? We have to move in the world, remembering God. Misfortunes may come up, so what? We shall meet them courageously. Sure enough we can rejoice and be happy if we have love for all.

I had gone to Rameshwaram to have a glimpse of the Lord Shiv. I was given a feeling that I might find the Lord there. Highly interested, I was moving towards the temple. But, what did I see? On the temple on a pole, it was written, "God is not here. He is within you." I lost my enthusiasm with which I was running fast towards the temple when a feeling dawned that I cannot see the Lord. But when I went inside and saw the statue of Lord Shiv there was a lot of satisfaction. It did give me a feeling that the Lord was there watching me lovingly. The Lord seem to say, "I was waiting for you to come."

"Remember the first thing that you should not forget is that our right is only to act. We have no power on the result of our actions. Our concern should be how we act always remembering the Lord."

My own experience in life has shown me this truth. I worked as a family member to carry out in starting a school and earn a lot of money and become rich and prosperous but I landed in serious financial crises, disgrace and defamation. I worked in a most disinterested manner by writing a book of short stories for the young ones, least bothered to succeed, only to find some little engagement and I succeeded in making a means to earn some good amount of money. Thereby, it is my firm belief that to act is in our hands, remembering God and moving in the right spirit. Whatever we do, we need to do it in the best way. That it is a prayer to the Lord. It is the feeling behind the action which is the most important thing. An action may be very simple but it assumes a stature of sublimity by the feeling behind it.

What is the difference between school life and life? In school life, you are taught a lesson and then given a test. But in life you are given a test that teaches you a lesson. Life is our teacher. Life communicates with us all the time and it is a lesson to see how life continuously has led me to the people I need to experience and to the places where I need to be.

I seek your blessings, I am not afraid, for you are near me and no harm can come to me. In this lonely life you have given me the strength to traverse a difficult path. When others left me, you were always by my side. I love you. God is love. The lovely flowers as they bloom and spread its scent all round is a great asset. "You are the world", has been aptly said by Krishnamurthy. Build your foundation in your heart. Your response to all those who meet you should be "I love you". If each one of us makes the beginning with oneself, the face of the world would change.

"Faith is the bird that sings when the dawn is still dark."

"I have put my faith in my Mother Divine. It has given me courage, immense courage. When fear lurks in my heart, it is faith that sets me free from distress. My Divine Ma loves me and with that I can accomplish the most difficult task. Her light continues to shine on me." All feelings like weak feelings cannot be termed as faith. It is only the strong feelings that can be termed as faith. Your faith can be in God or in Devil. Feelings turned into faith provide a foundation on which to base our life. It is on faith in high principles or in good people or in high ideas that we are apt to become sound and sensible people.

Sage Ved Vyas was given a unique assignment. He was asked to study all the spiritual and philosophical literature and sum up them in short. After intense study he issued one line, "The act of greatest merit is to help others and not to cause intentional pain to others." A loving word, a compassionate look and a simple good deed – all these can bring light to the life of less fortunate as well as your own. It is not what you gain but what you are able to give that determines the value of your life. You are blessed if you can give happiness to a soul. Compassion closely connected to friendship is what Ma seeks in Her devotees.

Ego is the greatest hindrance on the path of love. It is very important that you learn to crush it. What is ego? When you question "Who am I?" the ego answers in no time "I am the master of all I survey." "Every one should serve me." Or "no one is better than me." This is what we call false ego. This needs to be crushed. However, if you get the answer "You are here to serve others." It is a simple ego and must be developed so that you can spread love all round.

There should be a balance between happiness and sorrow. They pass away and you are not bothered. But the highest quality is that of forgiveness. Create an abundance of this quality. This is the greatest armour in the path of love.

Life moves on with all its pain and happiness. Permanence would mean paralysis. It is the heart that moves you, perhaps faster than movement. It is the heart that swells up, again it is the heart that pulls you down. Once, the tongue and the teeth had an argument. The teeth said, "I can bite you and finish you in no time." The tongue smiled and said that "I can speak such words for you that in no time you will be beaten so badly that only broken teeth will remain." Once with Gautam Buddha sat a man who kept on abusing Buddha. Buddha sat silently hearing him and after some time he asked his disciple who was also there to get some fruit and cut into pieces and give it to the one who was abusing him so that, "I return what he has given me."

Life is a gift given to man by God and we love life so much, life with its integral parts, emotions and feelings. Feelings of elation or depression, that of joys and sorrows spring out of the heart. With positive feelings you are apt to rise high but negative emotions hurl you to the ground and you are buried with shame and disgrace. As the thoughts are in the heart, so is the man. As the feelings grow up in the heart, it constitutes the personality of the person.

The first level of the heart is happy when it hears a sweet melody or views a good sight. It is confined to that moment and then forgotten. A beautiful sight touches the heart and music refreshes it. It stays for sometime only.

The second level of the heart is when one begins to seek happiness for others in which he feels lies his happiness also. He tries to work for others, to give inspiration to others towards a more meaningful life. He goes a little beyond his own self. Self-centredness begins to melt. Here there is power to think, to argue, to give lesson to others. He wants to build a structure on the foundation of his thoughts and actions for e.g., we have Kabir, Meera, Tulsidas, etc. to sing and inspire.

Happiness must be understood in the context of the word. We are facing situations that need a change drastically. Happiness, contentment through acceptance should be our goal towards a world with a new perspective for peace and prosperity. Acceptance of what is given to you forms a vital part of contentment. We need to see the smile on the face of a child which gives you contentment followed by happiness. It never comes with power. It gives smiles that enchants each and every soul. Power, position and money cannot help. "Happiness cannot be travelled to, earned, or consumed. Happiness is the spiritual experience of living every minute with love, grace, and gratitude."

Life is always in movement, moving with all its happiness and pain. God loved his creation and found this world for them to live in. But where was the place where He would sit with them, invisible yet visible. Heart was the right place for Him to live in. Keep your heart away from pride and selfishness. Otherwise, there will be no place for the Lord to sit on? It is the heart that swells up. Again, it is the heart that sinks you down. Feeling of elation or depression, that of joys and sorrows spring out of it. If the heart up-beats at times it sinks low on others. On other occasions you are impelled and elated by feelings for the welfare of the nation or the love of mankind, but at other times you go down with feelings of hatred, jealousy and revenge. So the heart is very unstable. One minute it may raise itself, and then it is thrown into mud again the next minute.

The glories of heart are tremendous. We are born with a heart that is pure. But as we grow up it begins to gather dust. We often fail in choosing the right direction. Unpleasant ideas and thoughts crop up. We more than often fail in choosing the right path.

It is your spiritual devotion which will make you the right person. Love makes its foundation in the heart. A spontaneous response towards anyone you meet should be that you love him. Make your heart run by using these words, then watch your result. Your life will brighten up with new love and understanding. Surrender yourself with new awareness and let love unfold within you.

To be friendly is another quality that you must inculcate. The bond of love should never diminish. You should chisel yourself constantly and then try to discard the ill feelings that may grow in you.

The Lord will be sitting within you if you have the quality to love others. It thus becomes a place for the Lord to reside in. The face of the world would be changed if each one us would have a heart full of love for others. Let us make a beginning. Your ready response with others when you meet with love will change the world. Paramhansa had so much of this quality within him that he would experience intense pain when he felt another's pain and sorrow. The great sages like Buddha give us inspiration.

It is the feeling behind the action which is the most important thing. An action may be very simple but it assumes a stature of sublimity by the feeling behind it. If a person's feeling is good, it makes the act extraordinary. Your actions become great because they are supplemented and seconded by noble thoughts. In your outlook, you are very humble.

A beautiful example cited would make my point clear. Pundalik, devoted to his old, disabled parents was once giving bath to his father. His service to his father was a worship to him. One day, the Lord appeared before him. Busy in giving his old father a bath he could not attend the Lord so he threw a brick, requested Him to sit as that moment belonged to his father and he could not spare even a minute for the Lord. The Lord smiling sat down and kept on watching Pundalik. When he finished his work and made his father sit comfortably on the bed, he turned towards the Lord to attend Him. The Lord was highly pleased to see his devotion and the spirit. See the same action of the sons today. Deprived of devotion, looking only for gains their action leads to their frustration, depression, unhappiness and regrets.

A boy was asked by his mother to go and see in the nearby house where his aunt has died as to what the ladies were saying about her.

The child ran to her house and saw how they were full of praise for her. Someone called her an angel while others narrated incidents of her kindness and love.

In a family that I recently visited there was so much love and understanding that it was a pleasure to be with them. Such moments are described by romantic poets like Shelley, Wordsworth and other poets. With love in our hearts and God seated there, we can hope for the best.

On the other hand, where does hatred lead us to? It takes us away from peace. Violence follows and that brings us to destruction. Why go for disappointments. Look for joy and happiness. If you have love, you have everything with music in life.

You have been sent to this world, not to renounce it but to

rejoice in it. The Lord has given the highest priority to actions. How can you then think of leaving this world? You were born here, so you must live here. You have to look at things with appreciation. Lord Krishna tells Arjun to face life and not to run away from it. If life is insecure, so what? You only have to face it courageously. You can rejoice and be happy if you have learnt the lesson to act with love for one and all.

God wanted to create something really beautiful and interesting. He looked around to find something of His choice. Failing in His intense desire, He created the world out of His very self. This is the real essence of Gita. *(Chapter 7, sloka 19)*

Meaning that such a soul is very rare who has this vision, the vision of oneness. The Lord is to be seen in all. Like a seed He is there in everything. This point of His presence in all has been stressed again and again.

God has created this world, so He loves so much to come to this world and be with what He has created. The great book GITA tells us to always remember Him. Though the Lord divided Himself, He told us, "Never to forget Me."

He is alone, who tell us, "Never forget Me." Though He divided His

Self with us, yet He stands alone as One. Nothing exists without Him. He multiplied and became many. But actually, He stands as One and undivided.

One who loves God must also love all that is His. He shines in all, therefore all require our feelings of love. The feelings, love and God, therefore become synonymous. So, we say God is love. He is sitting in our hearts. To awaken ourselves to this reality is to feel His presence.

To change the face of the world, all of us is responsible. I have to see that I am on the right path. Each one of us has to see that we are on the right path or not. Try to understand what the right path is and what qualities the right man should possess. If you love God, you will see Him in His creation. With this new understanding, your life will brighten up.

To be friendly is another quality. Love between each other should never diminish. You should constantly try to discard ill feelings that may grow up. The act of greatest merit is to help others and the greatest sin is to cause intentional pain to others. A loving word, a compassionate look and a simple good deed – all these can bring light to the lives of the less fortunate, as well as to your own. If you can bring happiness into the life of a single soul, it makes your life blessed.

Compassion is closely connected to friendship – this is what is needed. Hate and violence cannot lead you far. You will not be judged by how much faith you have in God. Compassion shows the man. It is the highest manifestation of love. If you claim to love God, and neglect this aspect of life that is compassion, you are not in any way near God. Love has no cause. In love you sacrifice all. You receive only to give.

Our aim in the world is to achieve happiness and must overshadow our miseries and sorrow. If this is our goal, love has to be our guide. In speech, in action, or in thought, if we put the lord before us, I am sure this world would be better than heaven.

The famous poet Shakespeare tells us that "Life is an empty dream. It is a stage where we come, tret and fret our feet and then move finally off and fall down from the stage never to be heard of again." This is not at all understanding life and its purpose. We are mistaken.

Let us have faith in the words of God and try to understand that we are bound to each other and bound to Him. We should not confine love to only the near and dear ones. It should be extended to all. The wicked and the cruel should not be left out. All of us can admire and love Ram, but our real test is when we can love Ravan also. Both the saint and the wicked are His manifestations. The whole world is like a family. You come to this world to act and rejoice. Life has a meaning and significance that cannot be overlooked. You enter this world to give, to act, and to rejoice in it. These are the words of Lord Krishna in Gita.

We have men who act so as to amass wealth, and rejoice in it. Their pleasure is in acquiring higher positions because for them "Enough is never quite enough." They attain victory often by dishonest means which in itself is a defeat.

They are self-centred, egoistic, and selfish in their behaviour.

Their pride makes them to crave for honours from others as their source of happiness. They seem to rejoice momentary and outwardly. But finally, they arrive to a state of disappointment and frustration. They have no faith in God as they consider their own selves as God. They do not believe in charity. They feel all belong to them they are the only ones that must enjoy and rejoice it in this world. They act, not with love, but with their eyes always fixed on the consequences of their action. They live and rejoice in a world of falsehood and feel that they are the happiest. But the truth they do realise later or sooner. They completely forget that they are of GOD and ignore the fact that they have come into the world with the mission; to live, to love and to remember the source from where they have come.

But life is music to those who have learnt to live and rejoice in the right way. Life needs to be lived by right actions, never for a moment forgetting the Lord. It is in surrendering to Him and then rejoicing that your life assumes importance. You must realise, it is you, who can individually make the difference by following a path of righteousness and truth. Make yourself feel special by serving no one but truth and

God. You will live to rejoice in this world.

Lewis points out, “The tragedy of life is not that it ends soon, but we wait so long to begin it.” So, begin fast. With faith in God, you should be courageous enough to begin and take the right path, however risky it may be. You have to give up anger and pride and free yourself from worldly bondages. No sorrow can befall those who never try to possess people and things as their own. Turn to Tagore, who found amidst the light and shade in the soul, music playing with which he loved the earth and rejoice being in it.

Understand life and rejoice in it, but learn to rejoice in the right way. A glass contained a sweet drink, which you wanted very much as you were very thirsty. But the glass was very beautiful and looking at it, you forgot the drink, and got completely absorbed in admiring the glass, its colour and design. Now, if the drink is life and glass the lust for money, power, and position, you are overlooking the essence.

We have been visiting the temples. We have taken their refuge but without getting even a glimpse of the Lord. In fact, He is not to be sought there, but in our hearts. He is within us. The minute we understand this, we will find Him not only within us but can see Him in every nook and corner of this world.

We need to have a spiritual pause. We have to get out of the hustle and bustle of the world. We have to ask ourselves certain questions. Keen inquisitiveness on our part is needed to obtain the answers to some questions. "Who am I?" "Where have I come from?" and "Where will I go?" If this state of enquiry is not there, we can never understand the divinity that is very much within us.

In the end, I must say that fearlessness must come in the devotee of the Lord. It is the fear that makes us tell lies and keeps us away from good actions. Let us be brave and not scared of family, society or death. Let us then walk with confidence in ourselves and our head held high as the Lord is sitting within us.

As we conclude this exploration, let us be reminded of the power of love in our lives. Love is a force that has the capacity to transform, heal, and bring meaning to our existence. It is a guiding principle that can inspire us to treat others with compassion, kindness, and empathy. It is a unifying force that can bridge divides, foster harmony, and promote understanding among people of diverse backgrounds and beliefs.